ORNAMENTS
to crochet 3 WAYS

Oh, what fun it is to crochet a sleighful of festive Christmas ornaments!
And it's especially delightful to create these happy designs in three different sizes—just choose from
worsted weight yarn, sport weight yarn, or cotton thread. If you can work a slip stitch, single crochet,
and double crochet, you can create all of these designs. Bells, pom-poms, beads, and other
small items are added for quick color and enchanting detail. And because these designs
are simple, you can make plenty of decorations before the holidays arrive!

Worsted
Weight

LEISURE ARTS, INC.
Little Rock, AR

Cotton Thread

Sport Weight

Ski Hat

■■□□ EASY

● **WORSTED WEIGHT YARN:** MEDIUM 4
   Color A (Green) - 10 yards (9 meters)
   Color B (Red) - 10 yards (9 meters)
   Crochet hook, size H (5 mm)
   Yarn needle

▶ **Finished Size**
Approximately 4" (10 cm) high

SPORT WEIGHT YARN: FINE 2 ●
   Color A (Orange) - 9 yards (8 meters)
   Color B (Lime) - 9 yards (8 meters)
   Crochet hook, size F (3.75 mm)
   Yarn needle

Finished Size
Approximately 3" (7.5 cm) high

● **BEDSPREAD WEIGHT COTTON THREAD (SIZE 10):**
   Color A (Green) - 8 yards (7.5 meters)
   Color B (Red) - 6 yards (5.5 meters)
   Steel crochet hook, size 1 (2.75 mm)
   Tapestry needle
   Small purchased red pom-pom
   Craft glue

▶ **Finished Size**
Approximately 1¹/₂" (4 cm) high

Instructions continued on page 9

Wreath

EASY

WORSTED WEIGHT YARN: MEDIUM 4

15 yards (13.5 meters)
Crochet hook, size H (5 mm)
2" (5 cm) diameter Plastic ring
Yarn needle
15 miniature gold bells
Sewing thread and needle
1/2"w (12 mm) red ribbon

Finished Size
Approximately 3 3/4" (9.5 cm) diameter

SPORT WEIGHT YARN: FINE 2

14 yards (13 meters)
Crochet hook, size F (3.75 mm)
1" (2.5 cm) diameter Plastic ring
Yarn needle
Five miniature gold bells
Sewing thread and needle
1/4"w (7 mm) pink ribbon

Finished Size
Approximately 2 3/4" (7 cm) diameter

BEDSPREAD WEIGHT COTTON THREAD (SIZE 10):

15 yards (13.5 meters)
Steel crochet hook, size 1 (2.75 mm)
5/8" (16 mm) diameter Plastic ring
Tapestry needle
15 Small gold seed beads
Sewing thread and needle
1/16"w (1.5 mm) red ribbon

Finished Size
Approximately 1 1/2" (4 cm) diameter

Instructions continued on page 9.

Candy Cane

EASY

WORSTED WEIGHT YARN: MEDIUM 4

Color A (White) - 9 yards (8 meters)
Color B (Red) - 7 yards (6.5 meters)
Crochet hook, size H (5 mm)
Yarn needle
12" (30.5 cm) of green chenille stem
3/8" (10 mm) green ribbon

Finished Size
Approximately 5 1/2" (14 cm) high

SPORT WEIGHT YARN: FINE 2

Color A (Pink) - 8 yards (7.5 meters)
Color B (Lime) - 6 yards (5.5 meters)
Crochet hook, size F (3.75 mm)
Yarn needle
12" (30.5 cm) of green chenille stem
1/4" (7 mm) yellow ribbon

Finished Size
Approximately 4" (10 cm) high

BEDSPREAD WEIGHT COTTON THREAD (SIZE 10):

Color A (White) - 6 yards (5.5 meters)
Color B (Red) - 4 yards (3.5 meters)
Steel crochet hook, size 1 (2.75 mm)
Tapestry needle
12" (30.5 cm) of green plastic-coated craft wire
1/8" (3 mm) green ribbon

Finished Size
Approximately 2 1/2" (6.5 cm) high

Instructions continued on page 8.

Bell

EASY

WORSTED WEIGHT YARN:
14 yards (13 meters)
Crochet hook, size H (5 mm)
Yarn needle
$3/4$" (19 mm) diameter silver jingle bell

Finished Size
Approximately $3^{1}/_{4}$" (8.5 cm) high

SPORT WEIGHT YARN:
13 yards (12 meters)
Crochet hook, size F (3.75 mm)
Yarn needle
$1/2$" (12 mm) diameter silver jingle bell

Finished Size
Approximately $2^{3}/_{4}$" (9.5 cm) high

BEDSPREAD WEIGHT COTTON THREAD (SIZE 10):
10 yards (9 meters)
Steel crochet hook, size 1 (2.75 mm)
Tapestry needle
$3/8$" (10 mm) diameter gold jingle bell

Finished Size
Approximately $1^{1}/_{2}$" (4 cm) high

Instructions continued on page 8.

Bell

continued from page 7

Work in Front Loops Only *(Fig. 1, page 31)* unless otherwise indicated.

BELL

Leaving a long end for sewing and hanger, ch 8.

Rnd 1 (Right side)**:** Being careful not to twist chain, slip st in Top Loop Only of first ch to form a ring *(Fig. 2, page 31)*; slip st in Top Loop Only of next 7 chs; place a marker to mark beginning of rnd *(see Markers, page 31)*: 8 sts.

Note: Loop a short piece of yarn/thread around any stitch to mark Rnd 1 as **right** side.

To increase, slip st in Back Loop Only of **next** st *(Fig. 1, page 31)*, then slip st in Front Loop Only of **same** st.

Rnd 2: Increase in each st around: 16 sts.

Rnd 3: Slip st in each st around.

Rnd 4: (Increase, slip st in next st) around: 24 sts.

Rnds 5-10: Slip st in each st around.

Rnd 11: (Increase, slip st in next 3 sts) around: 30 sts.

Rnd 12: Ch 1, **turn**; slip st in Back Loop Only of each st around; join with slip st to **both** loops of first st.

Rnds 13-16: Ch 1, turn; skip joining slip st, slip st in Back Loop Only of each st around; join with slip st to **both** loops of first st.

Finish off.

FINISHING

Weave long end through free loops of beginning ch *(Fig. 3, page 31)*; pull snug and secure end, do **not** cut yarn.

Hanger: With long end on **right** side, insert hook in loop of one st at top of Bell and pull up a loop with yarn/thread end; ch 6 using long end; finish off. Secure end of ch to Bell to form loop for hanger.

Clapper: Thread jingle bell onto yarn/thread. Leaving an 8" (20.5 cm) length, ch 11; slide bell up against last ch made, ch 11; finish off, leaving an 8" (20.5 cm) length. Attach ends of chain to inside top of Bell.

Flatten Bell with lower edge joining at center back.

Candy Cane

continued from page 6

CANDY CANE

With Color A and leaving a long end for sewing, ch 30.

Row 1 (Right side)**:** Sc in second ch from hook and each ch across; finish off: 29 sc.

Note: Loop a short piece of yarn/thread around any stitch to mark Row 1 as **right** side.

Rows 2 and 3: With **right** side facing, join Color B with sc in first sc *(see Joining With Sc, page 31)*; sc in each sc across; finish off.

Row 4: With **right** side facing, join Color A with sc in first sc; sc in each sc across; finish off.

FINISHING

Place chenille stem/craft wire down the **wrong** side of length of piece. Working through free loops of beginning ch *(Fig. 3, page 31)* and through **both** loops of sc on Row 4, whipstitch piece together *(Fig. 5, page 32)*, keeping chenille stem/craft wire inside tube. Cut chenille stem/craft wire slightly shorter than ends of piece. Twist tube to swirl stripes, then bend into Candy Cane shape.

Tie ribbon into a bow around Candy Cane.

Wreath

continued from page 5

Work in Front Loops Only *(Fig. 1, page 31)* unless otherwise indicated.

WREATH

Rnd 1 (Right side): Work 25 sc around plastic ring; join with slip st to Front Loop Only of first sc.

Note: Loop a short piece of yarn/thread around any stitch to mark **right** side.

Rnd 2: (Ch 5, slip st) 3 times in Front Loop Only of same sc and each sc around; finish off.

FINISHING

For worsted weight ornament, sew 5 groups of 3 miniature bells each to the Wreath.

For sport weight ornament, sew miniature bells to Wreath.

For thread ornament, sew 5 groups of 3 beads each to the Wreath.

Tie ribbon into a bow and tack to Wreath.

• •

Ski Hat

continued from page 4

Work in Front Loops Only *(Fig. 1, page 31)* unless otherwise indicated.

HAT

With Color A and leaving a long end for sewing, ch 10.

Rnd 1 (Right side): Being careful not to twist ch, slip st in Top Loop Only of first ch to form a ring *(Fig. 2, page 31)*; slip st in Top Loop Only of next 9 chs; place marker to mark beginning of rnd *(see Markers, page 31)*: 10 sts.

Note: Loop a short piece of yarn/thread around any stitch to mark Rnd 1 as **right** side.

To increase, slip st in Back Loop Only of **next** st *(Fig. 1, page 31)*, then slip st in Front Loop Only of **same** st.

Rnd 2: (Increase, slip st in next st) around: 15 sts.

Rnd 3: Slip st in each st around.

Rnd 4: (Increase, slip st in next 2 sts) around: 20 sts.

Rnd 5: Slip st in each st around.

Rnd 6: (Increase, slip st in next 3 sts) around: 25 sts.

Rnd 7: Slip st in each st around.

Rnd 8: (Increase, slip st in next 4 sts) around, changing to Color B in last st *(Fig. 4, page 31)*, do **not** cut Color A: 30 sts.

Rnd 9: Slip st in each st around, changing to Color A in last st; do **not** cut Color B.

Rnd 10: Slip st in each st around, changing to Color B in last st; do **not** cut Color A.

Rnds 11 and 12: Repeat Rnds 9 and 10; at end of Rnd 12, cut Color A.

Rnd 13: Slip st in each st around.

Rnds 14 and 15: Ch 1, **turn**; slip st in Back Loop Only of each st around; join with slip st in **both** loops of first slip st.

Finish off.

FINISHING

Weave long end through free loops of beginning ch *(Fig. 3, page 31)*; pull snug and secure end.

For worsted weight ornament, make a ³/₄" (19 mm) red Pom-Pom *(Figs. 6a-c, page 32)* and attach to top of Ski Hat.

For sport weight ornament, make a ¹/₂" (12 mm) lime Pom-Pom and attach to top of Ski Hat.

For thread ornament, glue purchased red pom-pom to top of Ski Hat.

Flatten Ski Hat with color changes at center back.

9

Snowman

 **EASY**

WORSTED WEIGHT YARN: **MEDIUM 4**
   Color A (White) - 21 yards (19 meters)
   Color B (Green) - 9 yards (8 meters)
   Color C (Red) - 9 yards (8 meters)
Crochet hook, size H (5 mm)
Small safety pin to use as a marker
Yarn needle
Cotton ball
Small amount of black felt
Two small purchased black pom-poms
Craft glue

▶ **Finished Size**
Approximately 6¹/₂" (16.5 cm) high

Worste

SPORT WEIGHT YARN: **FINE 2**
   Color A (Pink) - 20 yards (18.5 meters)
   Color B (Purple) - 8 yards (7.5 meters)
   Color C (Aqua) - 8 yards (7.5 meters)
Crochet hook, size F (3.75 mm)
Small safety pin to use as a marker
Yarn needle
Cotton ball
Small amount of yellow felt
Two small purchased yellow pom-poms
Craft glue

Sport

Finished Size
Approximately 5³/₄" (14.5 cm) high ◀

BEDSPREAD WEIGHT COTTON THREAD (SIZE 10):
  Color A (White) - 13 yards (12 meters)
  Color B (Green) - 6 yards (5.5 meters)
  Color C (Red) - 4 yards (3.5 meters)
Steel crochet hook, size 1 (2.75 mm)
Small safety pin to use as a marker
Tapestry needle
Small amount of fiberfill
Five small black seed beads
Sewing thread and needle
Small purchased red pom-pom
Craft glue

Finished Size
Approximately 2³/₄" (7 cm) high

Work in Front Loops Only *(Fig. 1, page 31)* unless otherwise indicated.

HEAD
With Color A and leaving a long end for sewing, ch 9.

Rnd 1 (Right side): Being careful not to twist chain, slip st in Top Loop Only of first ch to form a ring *(Fig. 2, page 31)*; slip st in Top Loop Only of next 8 chs; place marker to mark beginning of rnd *(see Markers, page 31)*: 9 sts.

Note: Loop a short piece of yarn/thread around any stitch to mark Rnd 1 as **right** side.

To increase, slip st in Back Loop Only of **next** st *(Fig. 1, page 31)*, then slip st in Front Loop Only of **same** st.

Rnd 2: Increase in each st around: 18 sts.

Rnds 3-5: Slip st in each st around.

To decrease, insert hook in Front Loop Only of each of next 2 sts, YO and draw through all 3 loops on hook **(counts as one slip st)**.

Rnd 6: (Decrease, slip st in next st) around: 12 sts.

Rnd 7: (Decrease, slip st in next st) around: 8 sts.

Rnd 8: Slip st in each st around.

Slip loop from hook onto safety pin to keep piece from unraveling while working the next step.

Weave long end through free loops of beginning ch *(Fig. 3, page 31)*; pull snug and secure end. Insert cotton ball/fiberfill into Head.

Place loop from safety pin back onto hook.

YOKE
Rnd 1: (Increase, slip st in next 3 sts) around: 10 sts.

Rnd 2: (Increase, slip st in next st) around: 15 sts.

Rnd 3: (Increase, slip st in next 2 sts) around: 20 sts.

Rnd 4: (Slip st in next 3 sts, increase) around: 25 sts.

Rnd 5: Slip st in next 2 sts, increase, (slip st in next 4 sts, increase) 4 times, slip st in next 2 sts: 30 sts.

Rnd 6: (Increase, slip st in next 5 sts) around: 35 sts.

Rnd 7: Slip st in next 4 sts, ch 1 (underarm), mark top loop of ch for st placement, skip next 8 sts, slip st in next 10 sts, ch 1 (underarm), mark top loop of ch for st placement, skip next 8 sts, slip st in next 5 sts; place marker around last st to mark center back: 19 sts and 2 chs.

Instructions continued on page 15.

Toy Soldier

 **EASY**

WORSTED WEIGHT YARN: **MEDIUM 4**
Color A (Blue) - 14 yards (13 meters)
Color B (Red) - 10 yards (9 meters)
Color C (White) - 9 yards (8 meters)
Color D (Yellow) - 8 yards (7.5 meters)
Crochet hook, size H (5 mm)
Small safety pin to use as marker
Yarn needle
Cotton ball
Two small purchased white pom-poms
Two small purchased black pom-poms
Craft glue

▶ **Finished Size**
Approximately 6¹/₂" (16.5 cm) high

SPORT WEIGHT YARN: **FINE 2**
Color A (Aqua) - 13 yards (12 meters)
Color B (Pink) - 9 yards (8 meters)
Color C (Lime) - 8 yards (7.5 meters)
Color D (Yellow) - 7 yards (6.5 meters)
Crochet hook, size F (3.75 mm)
Small safety pin to use as marker
Yarn needle
Cotton ball
Four small purple pom-poms
Craft glue

Finished Size
Approximately 5¹/₄" (13.5 cm) high ◀

BEDSPREAD WEIGHT COTTON THREAD (SIZE 10):
Color A (Blue) - 11 yards (10 meters)
Color B (Red) - 7 yards (6.5 meters)
Color C (White) - 5 yards (4.5 meters)
Color D (Yellow) - 4 yards (3.5 meters)
Steel crochet hook, size 1 (2.75 mm)
Small safety pin to use as marker
Tapestry needle
Small amount of fiberfill
Two small black seed beads
Two small white seed beads
Sewing thread and needle

▶ Finished Size
Approximately 2³/₄" (7 cm) high

Work in Front Loops Only *(Fig. 1, page 31)* unless otherwise indicated.

HEAD

With Color C and leaving a long end for sewing, ch 9.

Rnd 1 (Right side)**:** Being careful not to twist ch, slip st in Top Loop Only of first ch to form a ring *(Fig. 2, page 31)*, slip st in Top Loop Only of next 8 chs; place marker to mark beginning of rnd *(see Markers, page 31)*: 9 sts.

Note: Loop a short piece of yarn/thread around any stitch to mark Rnd 1 as **right** side.

To increase, slip st in Back Loop Only of **next** st *(Fig. 1, page 31)*, then slip st in Front Loop Only of **same** st.

Rnd 2: Increase in each st around: 18 sts.

Rnds 3-5: Slip st in each st around.

To decrease, insert hook in Front Loop Only of each of next 2 sts, YO and draw through all 3 loops on hook **(counts as one slip st)**.

Rnd 6: (Decrease, slip st in next st) around: 12 sts.

Rnd 7: (Decrease, slip st in next st) around: 8 sts.

Rnd 8: Slip st in each st around, changing to Color B in last st *(Fig. 4, page 31)*; cut Color C.

Slip loop from hook onto safety pin to keep piece from unraveling while working the next step.

Weave long end through free loops of beginning ch *(Fig. 3, page 31)*; pull snug and secure end. Tie loose ends of Colors B and C together and insert ends into head. Insert cotton ball/fiberfill into Head.

Place loop from safety pin back onto hook.

YOKE
Rnd 1: (Increase, slip st in next 3 sts) around: 10 sts.

Rnd 2: (Increase, slip st in next st) around: 15 sts.

Rnd 3: (Increase, slip st in next 2 sts) around: 20 sts.

Rnd 4: (Slip st in next 3 sts, increase) around: 25 sts.

Rnd 5: Slip st in next 2 sts, increase, (slip st in next 4 sts, increase) 4 times, slip st in next 2 sts: 30 sts.

Rnd 6: (Increase, slip st in next 5 sts) around; remove beginning rnd marker and slip st in next 9 sts, place marker around last st made to mark center back: 35 sts.

Rnd 7: Place marker to mark beginning of rnd, increase, slip st in next 3 sts, ch 1 (underarm), mark top loop of ch for st placement, skip next 8 sts, slip st in next 10 sts, ch 1 (underarm), mark top loop of ch for st placement, skip next 8 sts, slip st in next 5 sts, changing to Color A in last st: 20 slip sts and 2 chs.

Rnd 8: Slip st in each slip st and in bottom loop of each ch around: 22 sts.

Rnds 9 and 10: Slip st in each st around; do **not** finish off.

Instructions continued on page 14.

Toy Soldier

continued from page 13

FIRST LEG
Rnd 1: Slip st in next 11 sts, ch 1 (crotch), mark top loop of ch for st placement, skip next 11 sts, slip st in next st and mark last st made as first st of Rnd 2: 11 slip sts and 1 ch.

Rnd 2: Slip st in each slip st and in bottom loop of each ch around: 12 sts.

Rnds 3-5: Slip st in each st around.

Rnd 6: (Decrease, slip st in next 2 sts) around; finish off leaving a long end for sewing: 9 sts.

Weave long end through Front Loops Only of each st on Rnd 6; pull snug and secure end.

SECOND LEG
Rnd 1: With **right** side facing and Head away from you, join Color A with slip st in marked ch at crotch, remove marker; slip st in 11 skipped sts on Rnd 10 of Yoke; place marker to mark beginning of rnd: 12 sts.

First Leg may be pinned to back of Yoke to keep leg out of the way while working on the Second Leg.

Rnds 2-5: Slip st in each st around.

Rnd 6: (Decrease, slip st in next 2 sts) around; finish off leaving a long end for sewing: 9 sts.

Weave long end through Front Loops Only of each st on Rnd 6; pull snug and secure end.

ARM
Rnd 1: With **right** side facing and Head away from you, join Color B with slip st in marked ch at one underarm, remove marker; slip st in 8 skipped sts on Rnd 6 of Yoke; place marker to mark beginning of rnd: 9 sts.

Rnds 2-4: Slip st in each st around.

Finish off leaving a long end for sewing.

Weave long end through Front Loops Only of each st on Rnd 4; pull snug and secure end.

Repeat for Second Arm.

HAT
With Color A and leaving a long end for sewing, ch 9.

Rnd 1 (Right side)**:** Being careful not to twist ch, slip st in Top Loop Only of first ch to form a ring, slip st in Top Loop Only of next 8 chs; place marker to mark beginning of rnd: 9 sts.

Mark Rnd 1 as **right** side.

Rnd 2: Increase in each st around: 18 sts.

Rnds 3-6: Slip st in each st around.

Rnd 7: Ch 1, **turn**; slip st in Back Loop Only of each st around.

Rnd 8: Do **not** turn; slip st in Front Loop Only of each st around; mark last st made as center back, finish off.

Weave long end through free loops of beginning ch; pull snug and secure end.

FINISHING
BANDOLIER
With Color D, ch 40; finish off.

Wrap and tack bandolier around soldier.

For worsted weight ornament, cutting through loops on one end only, make a 3/4" (19 mm) yellow Pom-Pom *(Figs. 6a-c, page 32)* and attach to front of Hat. Place Hat over Head and tack or glue in place.

Glue purchased black pom-poms to Toy Soldier for eyes and white pom-poms to Toy Soldier for buttons.

For sport weight ornament, cutting through loops on one end only, make a 1/2" (12 mm) yellow Pom-Pom and attach to front of Hat. Place Hat over Head and tack or glue in place.

Glue purchased pom-poms to Toy Soldier for eyes and buttons.

For thread ornament, cutting through loops on one end only, make a 1/4" (7 mm) yellow Pom-Pom and attach to front of Hat. Place Hat over Head and tack or glue in place.

Sew white beads to Toy Soldier for buttons and black beads to Toy Soldier for eyes.

Snowman

continued from page 11

BODY

Rnd 1: Working in sts and in bottom loop of chs, (slip st in next 2 sts, increase) around: 28 sts.

Rnd 2: Slip st in each st around.

Rnd 3: (Increase, slip st in next 3 sts) around: 35 sts.

Rnd 4: Slip st in each st around.

Rnd 5: (Decrease, slip st in next 3 sts) around: 28 sts.

Rnd 6: Slip st in each st around.

Rnd 7: (Decrease, slip st in next 2 sts) around: 21 sts.

Rnd 8: Slip st in each st around.

Rnd 9: (Decrease, slip st in next st) around: 14 sts.

Rnd 10: Decrease around; finish off leaving a long end for sewing: 7 sts.

Weave long end through Front Loops only of each st on Rnd 10; pull snug and secure end.

ARMS

Rnd 1: With **right** side facing and Head away from you, join Color A with slip st in marked ch at one underarm, remove marker; slip st in 8 skipped sts on Rnd 6 of Yoke; place marker to mark beginning of rnd: 9 sts.

Rnds 2-5: Slip st in each st around.

Finish off leaving a long end for sewing. Weave long end through Front Loops Only of each st on Rnd 5; pull snug and secure end.

Repeat for Second Arm.

HAT

With Color B and leaving a long end for sewing, ch 9.

Rnd 1 (Right side)**:** Being careful not to twist chain, slip st in Top Loop Only of first ch to form a ring; slip st in Top Loop Only of next 8 chs, place marker to mark beginning of rnd: 9 sts.

Mark Rnd 1 as **right** side.

Rnd 2: Increase in each st around: 18 sts.

Rnds 3-6: Slip st in each st around.

Rnd 7: Ch 1, **turn**; slip st in Back Loop Only of each st around.

Rnd 8: Do **not** turn; slip st in each st around; join with slip st in both loops of first st; mark last st made as center back, finish off.

Weave long end through free loops of beginning ch; pull snug and secure end.

SCARF

First Half (Right side)**:** With Color C, ch 20; working in Top Loops Only of chs, dc in fourth ch from hook, place marker around last dc to mark Top end, dc in next ch, hdc in next ch, sc in next ch, slip st in last 13 chs; do **not** finish off.

Second Half: Ch 7, dc in fourth ch from hook and in next ch, hdc in next ch, sc in last ch, slip st in free loops of first ch; finish off.

FINISHING

Wrap and glue Scarf around neck with **right** side of both Scarf ends facing.

For worsted weight ornament, make a 3/4" (19 mm) red Pom-Pom **(Figs. 6a-c, page 32)** and attach to top of Hat. Place Hat over Head and tack or glue in place.

Cut three small squares from black felt. Glue to front of Snowman for buttons. Glue purchased black pom-poms to Snowman for eyes.

For sport weight ornament, make a 1/2" (12 mm) aqua Pom-Pom and attach to top of Hat. Place the Hat over Head with joining at center back. Tack or glue Hat in place.

Cut three small squares from yellow felt. Glue to front of Snowman for buttons. Glue purchased yellow pom-poms to Snowman for eyes.

For thread ornament, glue purchased red pom-pom to top of Hat. Place the Hat over Head with joining at center back. Tack or glue Hat in place.

Sew three beads to front of Snowman for buttons and two beads to Snowman for eyes.

Sweater

WORSTED WEIGHT YARN: MEDIUM 4
   20 yards (18.5 meters)
Crochet hooks, sizes G (4 mm)
  and H (5 mm)
Small safety pin to use as a marker
Yarn needle
Three red buttons
Sewing thread and needle
12" (30.5 cm) of green chenille stem

Finished Size
Approximately 3¹/₂" (9 cm) high

SPORT WEIGHT YARN: FINE 2
   19 yards (17.5 meters)
Crochet hooks, sizes E (3.5 mm) **and**
  F (3.75 mm)
Small safety pin to use as a marker
Yarn needle
Orange button
Sewing thread and needle
12" (30.5 cm) of orange chenille stem

Finished Size
Approximately 2¹/₄" (5.75 cm) high

BEDSPREAD WEIGHT COTTON THREAD (SIZE 10):
14 yards (13 meters)
Steel crochet hooks, sizes 1 (2.75 mm) **and** 2 (2.25 mm)
Small safety pin to use as a marker
Tapestry needle
15 small red seed beads
Sewing thread and needle
12" (30.5 cm) of green plastic-coated craft wire

▶ **Finished Size**
Approximately 1¹/₂" (6.5 cm) high

Work in Front Loops Only **(Fig. 1, page 31)** and use larger size hook unless otherwise indicated.

YOKE
With larger size hook, ch 15.

Rnd 1 (Right side)**:** Being careful not to twist ch, slip st in Top Loop Only of first ch to form a ring **(Fig. 2, page 31)**; slip st in Top Loop Only of next 14 chs; place marker to mark beginning of rnd **(see Markers, page 31)**: 15 sts.

Note: Loop a short piece of yarn/thread around any stitch to mark Rnd 1 as **right** side.

To increase, slip st in Back Loop Only of **next** st **(Fig. 1, page 31)**, then slip st in Front Loop Only of **same** st.

Rnd 2: (Increase, slip st in next 2 sts) around: 20 sts.

Rnd 3: (Slip st in next 3 sts, increase) around: 25 sts.

Rnd 4: Slip st in next 2 sts, increase, (slip st in next 4 sts, increase) 4 times, slip st in next 2 sts: 30 sts.

Rnd 5: (Increase, slip st in next 5 sts) around: 35 sts.

Rnd 6: Slip st in next 3 sts, increase, (slip st in next 6 sts, increase) 4 times, slip st in next 3 sts, remove marker; slip st in next 7 sts, place marker around last st made to mark center back: 40 sts.

Slip loop from hook onto safety pin to keep piece from unraveling while working the next step.

Turn piece **wrong** side out and weave in yarn/thread end on **wrong** side; turn piece **right** side out.

Place loop from safety pin back onto hook.

Rnd 7: Slip st in next 6 sts, ch 1 (underarm), mark top loop of ch for st placement, skip next 8 sts, slip st in next 12 sts, ch 1 (underarm), mark top loop of ch for st placement, skip next 8 sts, slip st in next 6 sts; place marker to mark beginning of rnd: 24 sts and 2 chs.

BODY
Rnd 1: Slip st in each slip st and in Bottom Loop Only of each ch around: 26 sts.

Rnds 2-7: Slip st in each st around.

Rnds 8 and 9: With smaller size hook, slip st in Back Loop Only of each st around.

Finish off.

RIGHT SLEEVE
Rnd 1: With larger size hook, **right** side facing, and neck at top, join yarn with slip st in marked ch at underarm on the right, remove marker; slip st in the 8 skipped sts on Rnd 6 of Yoke; place marker to mark beginning of rnd: 9 sts.

Rnds 2-6: Slip st in each st around.

Instructions continued on page 28.

Ice Skate

● **WORSTED WEIGHT YARN:**
   12 yards (11 meters)
   Crochet hook, size H (5 mm)
   Small safety pin to use as a marker
   Yarn needle
   12" (30.5 cm) of green chenille stem
   Craft glue

▶ **Finished Size**
   Approximately 3" (7.5 cm) high

SPORT WEIGHT YARN:
   11 yards (10 meters)
   Crochet hook, size F (3.75 mm)
   Small safety pin to use as a marker
   Yarn needle
   12" (30.5 cm) of lime chenille stem
   Craft glue

Finished Size
Approximately 2¹/₂" (6.5 cm) high ◀

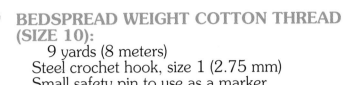

BEDSPREAD WEIGHT COTTON THREAD (SIZE 10):
9 yards (8 meters)
Steel crochet hook, size 1 (2.75 mm)
Small safety pin to use as a marker
Tapestry needle
12" (30.5 cm) of green plastic-coated craft wire
Craft glue

Finished Size
Approximately 1¹/₂" (4 cm) high

Work in Front Loops Only **(Fig. 1, page 31)** unless otherwise indicated.

TOE

Leaving a long end for sewing, ch 7.

Rnd 1 (Right side)**:** Being careful not to twist chain, slip st in Top Loop Only of first ch to form a ring **(Fig. 2, page 31)**; slip st in Top Loop Only of next 6 chs; place marker to mark beginning of rnd **(see Markers, page 31)**: 7 sts.

Note: Loop a short piece of yarn/thread around any stitch to mark Rnd 1 as **right** side.

To increase, slip st in Back Loop Only of **next** st **(Fig. 1, page 31)**, then slip st in Front Loop Only of **same** st.

Rnd 2: Increase in each st around: 14 sts.

Rnds 3-7: Slip st in each st around.

Rnd 8: (Increase, slip st in next 6 sts) twice: 16 sts.

Rnd 9: Slip st in each st around.

Slip loop from hook onto safety pin to keep piece from unraveling while working the next step.

Turn Toe **wrong** side out and weave long end through free loops of beginning ch **(Fig. 3, page 31)**; pull snug and secure end; turn Toe **right** side out.

Place loop from safety pin back onto hook.

HEEL

To work Heel Stitch A, insert hook in single loop at edge of previous row **and** in Front Loop Only of next st on Toe, YO and draw through all 3 loops on hook **(counts as one slip st)**.

To work Heel Stitch B, insert hook in single loop at edge of previous row **and** in Back Loop Only of next st on Toe, YO and draw through all 3 loops on hook **(counts as one slip st)**.

Row 1: Ch 1, **turn**; slip st in Back Loop Only of first 4 sts, leave remaining 12 sts unworked: 4 sts.

Row 2: Ch 1, turn; slip st in Front Loop Only of first 4 sts, work Heel St A: 5 sts.

Row 3: Ch 1, turn; slip st in Back Loop Only of first 5 sts, work Heel St B: 6 sts.

Row 4: Ch 1, turn; slip st in Front Loop Only of first 6 sts, work Heel St A: 7 sts.

Row 5: Ch 1, turn; slip st in Back Loop Only of first 7 sts, work Heel St B: 8 sts.

Row 6: Ch 1, turn; slip st in Front Loop Only first 8 sts, work Heel St A: 9 sts.

Row 7: Ch 1, turn; slip st in Back Loop Only of first 9 sts, work Heel St B: 10 sts.

Instructions continued on page 28.

Santa

EASY

WORSTED WEIGHT YARN: **MEDIUM 4**
Color A (White) - 23 yards (21 meters)
Color B (Red) - 15 yards (13.5 meters)
Color C (Green) - 9 yards (8 meters)
Crochet hook, size H (5 mm)
Yarn needle
Two small purchased black pom-poms
Craft glue

Finished Size
Approximately 5¹/₂" (14 cm) high

Worsted

Sport

SPORT WEIGHT YARN: **FINE 2**
Color A (Pink) - 21 yards (19 meters)
Color B (Yellow) - 13 yards (12 meters)
Color C (Lime) - 7 yards (6.5 meters)
Crochet hook, size F (3.75 mm)
Yarn needle
Two small purchased blue pom-poms
Craft glue

Finished Size
Approximately 4¹/₂" (11.5 cm) high

BEDSPREAD WEIGHT COTTON THREAD (SIZE 10):
Color A (White) - 13 yards (12 meters)
Color B (Red) - 8 yards (7.5 meters)
Color C (Green) - 4 yards (3.5 meters)
Steel crochet hook, size 1 (2.75 mm)
Tapestry needle
Two small black seed beads
Sewing needle and thread
Small green purchased pom-pom
Small red purchased pom-pom
Craft glue

Finished Size
Approximately 2¼" (5.75 cm) high

Work in Front Loops Only *(Fig. 1, page 31)* unless otherwise indicated.

CIRCLE (Make 2)
With Color A and leaving a long end for sewing, ch 12.

Rnd 1 (Right side): Being careful not to twist ch, slip st in Top Loop Only of first ch to form a ring *(Fig. 2, page 31)*, slip st in Top Loop Only of next 11 chs; place marker to mark beginning of rnd *(see Markers, page 31)*: 12 sts.

Note: Loop a short piece of yarn/thread around any stitch to mark Rnd 1 as **right** side.

To increase, slip st in Back Loop Only of **next** st *(Fig. 1, page 31)*, then slip st in Front Loop Only of **same** st.

Rnd 2: Increase in each st around: 24 sts.

Rnd 3: Slip st in each st around.

Rnd 4: (Increase, slip st in next st) around: 36 sts.

Rnd 5: Slip st in each st around.

Rnd 6: Slip st in Back Loop Only of each st around; finish off.

Weave long end through free loops of beginning ch *(Fig. 3, page 31)*; pull snug and secure end.

On one of the Circles, mark the Front Loop Only of the seventh st on Rnd 5 for st placement.

With **wrong** sides together and working through **both** loops on **both** pieces, whipstitch the circles together *(Fig. 5, page 32)*.

BEARD
With **right** side of marked Circle facing, marked st at top, and working in free loops of sts on Rnd 5, join Color A with slip st in marked st (remove marker); (ch 5, slip st) twice in same st and next 23 sts; finish off.

HAT
With Color B and leaving a long end for sewing, ch 4.

Rnd 1 (Right side): Being careful not to twist ch, slip st in Top Loop Only of first ch to form a ring, slip st in Top Loop Only of next 3 chs; place marker to mark beginning of rnd: 4 sts.

Mark Rnd 1 as **right** side.

Rnd 2: (Increase, slip st in next st) twice: 6 sts.

Rnd 3: Slip st in each st around.

Rnd 4: (Increase, slip st in next st) around: 9 sts.

Rnd 5: Slip st in each st around.

Rnd 6: (Increase, slip st in next 2 sts) around: 12 sts.

Rnd 7: Slip st in each st around.

Rnd 8: (Increase, slip st in next 2 sts) around: 16 sts.

Rnd 9: Slip st in each st around.

Rnd 10: (Increase, slip st in next 3 sts) around: 20 sts.

Rnds 11: Slip st in each st around.

Rnd 12: (Increase, slip st in next 4 sts) around: 24 sts.

Rnds 13 and 14: Slip st in each st around.

Instructions continued on page 28.

Angel

 EASY

WORSTED WEIGHT YARN: MEDIUM 4
    Color A (White) - 19 yards (17.5 meters)
    Color B (Gold) - 8 yards (7.5 meters)
Crochet hook, size H (5 mm)
Cotton ball
Yarn needle
³/₈" (10 mm) white ribbon

▶ **Finished Size**
Approximately 5¹/₂" (14 cm) high

SPORT WEIGHT YARN: FINE 2
    Color A (Pink) - 18 yards (16.5 meters)
    Color B (Orange) - 7 yards (6.5 meters)
Crochet hook, size F (3.75 mm)
Cotton ball
Yarn needle
¹/₄" (7 mm) orange ribbon

Finished Size
Approximately 4¹/₄" (11 cm) high ◀

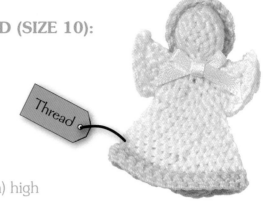

BEDSPREAD WEIGHT COTTON THREAD (SIZE 10):
Color A (White) - 11 yards (10 meters)
Color B (Gold) - 5 yards (4.5 meters)
Steel crochet hook, size 1 (2.75 mm)
Tapestry needle
Cotton ball
¹/₈" (3 mm) Ribbon

Finished Size
Approximately 2" (5 cm) high

Work in Front Loops Only *(Fig. 1, page 31)* unless otherwise indicated.

HEAD
With Color A and leaving a long end for sewing, ch 7.

Rnd 1 (Right side)**:** Being careful not to twist ch, slip st in Top Loop Only of first ch to form a ring *(Fig. 2, page 31)*, slip st in Top Loop Only of next 6 chs; place marker to mark beginning of rnd *(see Markers, page 31)*: 7 sts.

Note: Loop a short piece of yarn/thread around any stitch to mark Rnd 1 as **right** side.

To increase, slip st in Back Loop Only of **next** st *(Fig. 1, page 31)*, then slip st in Front Loop Only of **same** st.

Rnd 2: Increase in each st around: 14 sts.

Rnds 3-5: Slip st in each st around.

To decrease, insert hook in Front Loop Only of each of next 2 sts, YO and draw through all 3 loops on hook **(counts as one slip st)**.

Rnd 6: Decrease around: 7 sts.

Rnds 7 and 8: Slip st in each st around; do **not** finish off.

YOKE
Rnd 1: Increase in each st around: 14 sts.

Rnd 2: (Slip st in next st, increase) around: 21 sts.

Rnd 3: (Increase, slip st in next 2 sts) around: 28 sts.

Rnd 4: (Slip st in next st, increase) around: 42 sts.

Rnd 5: Slip st in each st around.

Rnd 6: Slip st in next 5 sts, skip next 12 sts (armhole), slip st in next 9 sts, skip next 12 sts (armhole), slip st in next 4 sts; do **not** finish off: 18 sts.

SKIRT
Rnd 1: (Increase, slip st in next 5 sts) around: 21 sts.

Rnd 2: Slip st in each st around.

Rnd 3: (Increase, slip st in next 6 sts) around: 24 sts.

Rnd 4: Slip st in each st around.

Rnd 5: (Increase, slip st in next 7 sts) around: 27 sts.

Rnd 6: Slip st in each st around.

Rnd 7: (Increase, slip st in next 8 sts) around: 30 sts.

Rnd 8: Slip st in next 8 sts, changing to Color B in last st made *(Fig. 4, page 31)*, finish off Color A; mark st below last st made as center back.

Rnd 9: Slip st in each st around.

Rnd 10: Ch 1, turn; slip st in each st around.

Instructions continued on page 29.

Stocking

■■□□ EASY

Worsted

- **WORSTED WEIGHT YARN:** **MEDIUM 4**
    Color A (Red) - 13 yards (12 meters)
    Color B (White) - 8 yards (7.5 meters)
  Crochet hook, size H (5 mm)
  Small safety pin to use as a marker
  Yarn needle

▶ **Finished Size**
Approximately 6" (15 cm) high

Sport

SPORT WEIGHT YARN: **FINE 2**
    Color A (Purple) - 12 yards (11 meters)
    Color B (Aqua) - 7 yards (6.5 meters)
  Crochet hook, size F (3.75 mm)
  Small safety pin to use as a marker
  Yarn needle

Finished Size
Approximately 4¹/₂" (11.5 cm) high

BEDSPREAD WEIGHT COTTON THREAD (SIZE 10):
Color A (Red) - 8 yards (7.5 meters)
Color B (White) - 6 yards (5.5 meters)
Steel crochet hook, size 1 (2.75 mm)
Small safety pin to use as a marker
Tapestry needle

Finished Size
Approximately 2¹/₄" (5.75 cm) high

Work in Front Loops Only *(Fig. 1, page 31)* unless otherwise indicated.

TOE
With Color A and leaving a long end for sewing, ch 8.

Rnd 1 (Right side)**:** Being careful not to twist ch, slip st in Top Loop Only of first ch to form a ring *(Fig. 2, page 31)*; slip st in Top Loop Only of next 7 chs; place marker to mark beginning of rnd *(see Markers, page 31)*: 8 sts.

Note: Loop a short piece of yarn/thread around any stitch to mark Rnd 1 as **right** side.

To increase, slip st in Back Loop Only of **next** st *(Fig. 1, page 31)*, then slip st in Front Loop Only of **same** st.

Rnd 2: Increase in each st around: 16 sts.

Rnds 3-8: Slip st in each st around.

Slip loop from hook onto safety pin to keep piece from unraveling while working the next step.

Turn Toe **wrong** side out and weave long end through free loops of beginning ch *(Fig. 3, page 31)*; pull snug and secure end; turn Toe **right** side out.

Place loop from safety pin back onto hook.

HEEL
To work Heel Stitch A, insert hook in single loop at edge of previous row **and** in Front Loop Only of next st on Toe, YO and draw through all 3 loops on hook **(counts as one slip st)**.

To work Heel Stitch B, insert hook in single loop at edge of previous row **and** in Back Loop Only of next st on Toe, YO and draw through all 3 loops on hook **(counts as one slip st)**.

Row 1: Ch 1, **turn**; slip st in Back Loop Only of first 4 sts: 4 sts.

Row 2: Ch 1, turn; slip st in Front Loop Only of first 4 sts, work Heel St A: 5 sts.

Row 3: Ch 1, turn; slip st in Back Loop Only of first 5 sts, work Heel St B: 6 sts.

Row 4: Ch 1, turn; slip st in Front Loop Only of first 6 sts, work Heel St A: 7 sts.

Row 5: Ch 1, turn; slip st in Back Loop Only of first 7 sts, work Heel St B: 8 sts.

Row 6: Ch 1, turn; slip st in Front Loop Only of first 8 sts, work Heel St A: 9 sts.

Row 7: Ch 1, turn: slip st in Back Loop Only of first 9 sts, work Heel St B: 10 sts.

Row 8: Ch 1, turn; working in Front Loops Only, slip st in first st, mark st just made for st placement, slip st in next 9 sts, work Heel St A; working in last 5 sts of Toe, slip st in next st, (increase, slip st in next st) twice; place marker to mark beginning of rnd: 18 sts.

TOP
Rnd 1: Insert hook in one loop at edge of row below marked st (at beginning of Row 8) and in Front Loop Only of marked st, YO and draw through all 3 loops on hook, **(counts as one slip st)**, remove marker from marked st, slip st in next 17 sts.

Instructions continued on page 29.

Gingerbread Man

▭▭☐☐ EASY

WORSTED WEIGHT YARN: MEDIUM 4
  21 yards (19 meters)
Crochet hook, size H (5 mm)
Small safety pin to use as marker
Yarn needle
Five small purchased white pom-poms
3" (7.5 cm) of white chenille stem
3/8" (10 mm) red ribbon
Craft glue

Finished Size
Approximately 5 1/2" (14 cm) high

SPORT WEIGHT YARN: FINE 2
  18 yards (16.5 meters)
Crochet hook, size F (3.75 mm)
Small safety pin to use as marker
Yarn needle
Five small purchased orange pom-poms
3" (7.5 cm) of orange chenille stem
1/4" (7 mm) yellow ribbon
Craft glue

Finished Size
Approximately 4"
(10 cm) high

BEDSPREAD WEIGHT COTTON THREAD (SIZE 10):
  11 yards (10 meters)
Steel crochet hook, size 1 (2.75 mm)
Small safety pin to use as marker
Tapestry needle
Five small gold seed beads
Sewing needle and thread
Brown embroidery floss
1/16" (1.5 mm) red ribbon
Craft glue

Finished Size
Approximately 2" (5 cm) high

26

Work in Front Loops Only *(Fig. 1, page 31)* unless otherwise indicated.

HEAD

Leaving a long end for sewing, ch 9.

Rnd 1 (Right side)**:** Being careful not to twist ch, slip st in Top Loop Only of first ch to form a ring *(Fig. 2, page 31)*, slip st in Top Loop Only of next 8 chs; place marker to mark beginning of rnd *(see Markers, page 31)*: 9 sts.

Note: Loop a short piece of yarn/thread around any stitch to mark Rnd 1 as **right** side.

To increase, slip st in Back Loop Only of **next** st, then slip st in Front Loop Only of **same** st.

Rnd 2: Increase in each st around: 18 sts.

Rnds 3-5: Slip st in each st around.

To decrease, insert hook in Front Loop Only of each of next 2 sts, YO and draw through all 3 loops on hook **(counts as one slip st)**.

Rnd 6: (Decrease, slip st in next st) around: 12 sts.

Rnd 7: (Decrease, slip st in next st) around: 8 sts.

Rnd 8: Slip st in each st around.

Slip loop from hook onto safety pin to keep piece from unraveling while working the next step.

Weave long end through free loops of beginning ch *(Fig. 3, page 31)*; pull snug and secure end.

Place loop from safety pin back onto hook.

YOKE

Rnd 1: (Increase, slip st in next 3 sts) around: 10 sts.

Rnd 2: (Increase, slip st in next st) around: 15 sts.

Rnd 3: (Increase, slip st in next 2 sts) around: 20 sts.

Rnd 4: (Slip st in next 3 sts, increase) around: 25 sts.

Rnd 5: Slip st in next 2 sts, increase, (slip st in next 4 sts, increase) 4 times, slip st in next 2 sts: 30 sts.

Rnd 6: (Increase, slip st in next 5 sts) around, remove marker; slip st in next 9 sts, mark last st as center back, place marker to mark beginning of rnd: 35 sts.

Rnd 7: Increase, slip st in next 3 sts, ch 1 (underarm), mark top loop of ch for st placement, skip next 8 sts, slip st in next 10 sts, ch 1 (underarm), mark top loop of ch for st placement, skip next 8 sts, slip st in next 5 sts: 20 slip sts and 2 chs.

Rnd 8: Slip st in each slip st and in bottom loop of each ch around: 22 sts.

FIRST LEG

Rnd 1: Slip st in next 11 sts, ch 1 (crotch), mark top loop of ch for st placement, skip next 11 sts, slip st in next st and mark last st made as first st of Rnd 2: 11 slip sts and 1 ch.

Rnd 2: Slip st in each slip st and in bottom loop of each ch around: 12 sts.

Rnds 3-6: Slip st in each st around.

Rnd 7: (Decrease, slip st in next 2 sts) around; finish off leaving a long end for sewing: 9 sts.

Weave long end through Front Loops Only of each st on Rnd 7; pull snug and secure end.

SECOND LEG

Rnd 1: With **right** side facing and Head away from you, join yarn with slip st in marked ch at crotch, remove marker, slip st in 11 skipped sts on Rnd 8 of Yoke: 12 sts.

First Leg may be pinned to back of Yoke to keep leg out of the way while working on the Second Leg.

Rnds 2-6: Slip st in each st around.

Rnd 7: (Decrease, slip st in next 2 sts) around; finish off leaving a long end for sewing: 9 sts.

Weave long end through Front Loops Only of each st on Rnd 7; pull snug and secure end.

Instructions continued on page 29.

Sweater

continued from page 17

Rnd 7: Slip st in each st around, remove marker; slip st in next 6 sts, place marker to mark beginning of rnd.

Rnds 8 and 9: With smaller size hook, slip st in Back Loop Only of each st around.

Finish off.

LEFT SLEEVE
Rnd 1 (Right side)**:** With larger size hook, **right** side facing, and neck at top, join yarn with slip st in marked ch at underarm on the left, remove marker; slip st in the 8 skipped sts on Rnd 6 of Yoke, place marker to mark beginning of rnd: 9 sts.

Rnds 2-7: Slip st in each st around.

Rnds 8 and 9: With smaller size hook, slip st in Back Loop Only of each st around.

Finish off.

FINISHING
For worsted weight ornament, sew buttons to front of Sweater.

For sport weight ornament, sew button to front of Sweater.

For thread ornament, sew 3 groups of 3 beads each to front of Sweater.

Shape chenille stem/wire into hanger, trimming off any excess. Place Sweater on hanger.

Ice Skate

continued from page 19

Row 8: Ch 1, turn; slip st in Front Loop Only of first 10 sts, work Heel St A: 11 sts.

Row 9: Ch 1, turn; slip st in Back Loop Only of first 11 sts, work Heel St B: 12 sts.

Row 10: Ch 1, turn; working in Front Loops Only, slip st in first st, mark st just made for st placement, slip st in next 11 sts, work Heel St A, slip st in last 3 sts on Toe; place marker to mark beginning of rnd: 16 sts.

TOP
Rnd 1: Insert hook in one loop at edge of row **below** marked st (at beginning of Row 10) **and** in Front Loop Only of marked st, YO and draw through all 3 loops on hook **(counts as one slip st)**, remove marker from marked st, slip st in next 15 sts.

Rnds 2 and 3: Slip st in each st around.

Rnd 4: Slip st in each st around, remove marker; slip st in next 9 sts, place marker to mark beginning of rnd.

Rnd 5: Slip st in Back Loop Only of each st around; slip st in **both** loops of next st, finish off.

FINISHING
Flatten Ice Skate with top joining at edge.

Shape chenille stem/wire into a Blade, trimming off any excess. Insert ends of Blade into bottom of Skate, securing with craft glue.

Santa

continued from page 21

Rnd 15: Slip st in each st around, changing to Color C in last st *(Fig. 4, page 31)*; finish off Color B.

Rnd 16: Slip st in each st around.

Rnds 17 and 18: Slip st in Back Loop Only of each st around.

Finish off.

FINISHING
For worsted weight ornament, make a 3/4" (19 mm) green and a 3/4" red Pom-Pom *(Figs. 6a-c, page 32)*. Attach green pom-pom to tip of Hat. Place Hat over Head, fold to front, and tack or glue in place.

Attach red pom-pom to Santa just below center hole for nose. Glue purchased black pom-poms to Santa for eyes.

For sport weight ornament, make a 1/2" (12 mm) lime and a 1/2" yellow Pom-Pom. Attach lime pom-pom to tip of Hat. Place Hat over Head, fold to front, and tack or glue in place.

Attach yellow pom-pom to Santa just below center hole for nose. Glue purchased blue pom-poms to Santa for eyes.

For thread ornament, glue purchased green pom-pom to tip of Hat. Place Hat over Head, fold to front, and tack or glue in place.

Glue purchased red pom-pom to Santa just below center hole. Sew black beads to Santa for eyes.

Angel
continued from page 23

Slip st in Back Loop Only of each st around; join with slip st in **both** loops of first slip st.

Finish off.

WING
Row 1: With **right** side facing and working in skipped armhole sts, join Color A with slip st in second skipped st; slip st in next st, (increase, slip st in next st) 4 times, leave remaining st unworked: 14 sts.

Row 2: Ch 1, turn; slip st in Back Loop Only of next 14 sts and in next 2 skipped sts on Yoke; place marker to mark beginning of rnd: 16 sts.

Last Rnd: Do **not** turn; slip st in Back Loop Only of each st around; finish off.

Repeat for second Wing.

HALO
With Color B, ch 18; being careful not to twist ch, slip st in first ch to form a ring; slip st in next 17 chs; finish off.

FINISHING
Stuff the cotton ball/fiberfill into the Head through the top hole. Weave long end through free loops of beginning ch *(Fig. 3, page 31)*; pull snug and secure end.

Fit Halo around Head and tack in place.

Tie ribbon into a bow and tack to neck.

Stocking
continued from page 25

Rnd 2: Slip st in next 14 sts, increase twice, slip st in next 2 sts: 20 sts.

Rnd 3: Slip st in each st around.

Rnd 4: Slip st in next 16 sts, increase twice, slip st in next 2 sts: 22 sts.

Rnd 5: Slip st in each st around, changing to Color B in last st *(Fig. 4, page 31)*; finish off Color A, mark last st as center back.

CUFF
Rnd 1: Slip st in each st around.

Rnd 2: Ch 1, **turn**; slip st in Back Loop Only of each st around; slip st in **both** loops of next st.

Rnd 3: Ch 1, turn; slip st in Front Loop Only of each st around; join with slip st to **both** loops of first st.

Rnd 4: Ch 1, turn; slip st in Back Loop Only of each st around; join with slip st to **both** loops of first st.

Rnd 5: Ch 1, turn; slip st in Front Loop Only of each st around; join with slip st to **both** loops of first st.

Row 6: Ch 1, turn; slip st in Back Loop Only of each st around; join with slip st to **both** loops of first st, ch 7, slip st in same st as joining **(hanging loop made)**, finish off.

Flatten Stocking with hanging loop at edge.

Gingerbread Man
continued from page 27

ARM
Rnd 1: With **right** side facing and Head away from you, join yarn with slip st in marked ch at underarm, remove marker; slip st in 8 skipped sts on Rnd 6 of Yoke: 9 sts.

Rnds 2-4: Slip st in each st around.

Finish off leaving a long end for sewing.

Weave long end through Front Loops Only of each st on Rnd 4; pull snug and secure end.

Repeat for Second Arm.

FINISHING
For worsted weight and sport weight ornaments, glue purchased pom-poms to Gingerbread Man for eyes and buttons.

Shape chenille stem into a mouth, trimming off any excess. Glue mouth to Gingerbread Man below eyes.

For thread ornament, sew beads to Gingerbread Man for eyes and buttons.

Use embroidery floss to sew a mouth below Gingerbread Man's eyes.

Tie ribbon into a bow and tack to neck.

General Instructions

The instructions in this leaflet were written for use with worsted weight yarn in traditional Christmas colors and sizes G and H aluminum crochet hooks. For extra holiday pizzazz, try crocheting the ornaments with sport weight yarn in bright colors and size E and F aluminum crochet hooks as shown on page 3. Or, for a more delicate look, try making the ornaments with bedspread weight cotton thread and sizes 0 and 1 steel crochet hooks as shown on page 2. So, whatever your holiday style, these ornaments will make them merry!

ABBREVIATIONS

ch(s)　chain(s)
cm　centimeters
dc　double crochet(s)
hdc　half double crochet(s)
mm　millimeters
Rnd(s)　Round(s)
sc　single crochet(s)
st(s)　stitch(es)
YO　yarn over

( ) or [ ] — work enclosed instructions **as many** times as specified by the number immediately following **or** contains explanatory remarks.
colon (:) — the number(s) given after a colon at the end of a row or round denote(s) the number of stitches or spaces you should have on that row or round.

GAUGE

Gauge is not of great importance; your Ornaments may be a little larger or smaller without changing the overall effect.

HINTS

As in all crocheted pieces, good finishing techniques make a big difference in the quality of the piece.

Make a habit of taking care of loose ends as you work. Thread a yarn/tapestry needle with the yarn/thread end. With **wrong** side facing, weave the needle through several stitches, then reverse the direction and weave it back through several stitches. When ends are secure, clip them off close to work.

CROCHET TERMINOLOGY	
UNITED STATES	**INTERNATIONAL**
slip stitch (slip st) =	single crochet (sc)
single crochet (sc) =	double crochet (dc)
half double crochet (hdc) =	half treble crochet (htr)
double crochet (dc) =	treble crochet (tr)
treble crochet (tr) =	double treble crochet (dtr)
double treble crochet (dtr) =	triple treble crochet (ttr)
triple treble crochet (tr tr) =	quadruple treble crochet (qtr)
skip =	miss

Yarn Weight Symbol & Names	SUPER FINE 1	FINE 2	LIGHT 3	MEDIUM 4	BULKY 5	SUPER BULKY 6
Type of Yarns in Category	Sock, Fingering Baby	Sport, Baby	DK, Light Worsted	Worsted, Afghan, Aran	Chunky, Craft, Rug	Bulky, Roving
Crochet Gauge Ranges in Single Crochet to 4" (10 cm)	21-32 sts	16-20 sts	12-17 sts	11-14 sts	8-11 sts	5-9 sts
Advised Hook Size Range	B-1 to E-4	E-4 to 7	7 to I-9	I-9 to K-10.5	K-10.5 to M-13	M-13 and larger

CROCHET HOOKS												
U.S.	B-1	C-2	D-3	E-4	F-5	G-6	H-8	I-9	J-10	K-10½	N	P	Q
Metric - mm	2.25	2.75	3.25	3.5	3.75	4	5	5.5	6	6.5	9	10	15

STEEL CROCHET HOOKS															
U.S.	00	0	1	2	3	4	5	6	7	8	9	10	11	12	13	14
Metric - mm	3.5	3.25	2.75	2.25	2.1	2.1	2.1	1.8	1.65	1.5	1.4	1.3	1.1	1	.85	.75

MARKERS

Markers are used to help distinguish the beginning of each round being worked. Place a 2" (5 cm) scrap piece of yarn/thread before the first stitch of each round, moving marker after each round is completed.

JOINING WITH SC

When instructed to join with sc, begin with a slip knot on hook. Insert hook in stitch or space indicated, YO and pull up a loop, YO and draw through both loops on hook.

BACK OR FRONT LOOPS ONLY

Work only in loop(s) indicated by arrow *(Fig. 1)*.

Fig. 1

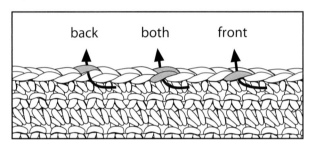

TOP LOOPS OF A CHAIN

When instructed to work in top loops of a chain, work in loop indicated by arrow *(Fig. 2)*.

Fig. 2

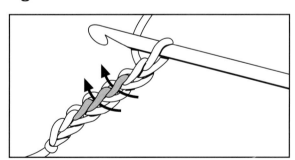

FREE LOOPS OF A CHAIN

When instructed to work in free loops of a chain, work in loop indicated by arrow *(Fig. 3)*.

Fig. 3

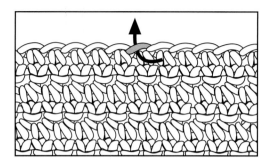

CHANGING COLORS

Work the last stitch to within one step of completion, hook new yarn *(Fig. 4)* and draw through all loops on hook.

Fig. 4

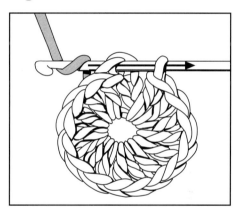

◕□□□ BEGINNER	Projects for first-time crocheters using basic stitches. Minimal shaping.
◕◕□□ EASY	Projects using yarn with basic stitches, repetitive stitch patterns, simple color changes, and simple shaping and finishing.
◕◕◕□ INTERMEDIATE	Projects using a variety of techniques, such as basic lace patterns or color patterns, mid-level shaping and finishing.
◕◕◕◕ EXPERIENCED	Projects with intricate stitch patterns, techniques and dimension, such as non-repeating patterns, multi-color techniques, fine threads, small hooks, detailed shaping and refined finishing.

WHIPSTITCH

Place **wrong** sides together and sew through both pieces/sides once to secure the beginning of the seam, leaving an ample yarn end to weave in later. Insert the needle from **front** to **back** through **both** loops on **both** pieces/sides *(Fig. 5)*. Bring the needle around and insert it from **front** to **back** through next loops of both pieces/sides. Continue in this manner around/across, keeping the sewing yarn fairly loose.

Fig. 5

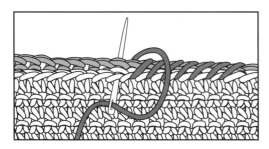

Fig. 6a

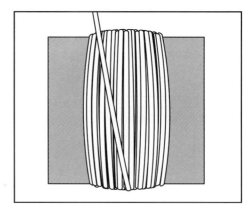

POM-POM

Cut a piece of cardboard 3" (7.5 cm) wide and as long as you want the diameter of your finished pom-pom to be.

Wind the yarn/thread around the cardboard until it is approximately ¹/₂" (12 mm) thick in the middle *(Fig. 6a)*.

Carefully slip the yarn/thread off the cardboard and firmly tie an 18" (45.5 cm) length of yarn/thread around the middle *(Fig. 6b)*. Leave yarn/thread ends long enough to attach the pom-pom. Cut the loops on both ends and trim the pom-pom into a smooth ball *(Fig. 6c)*.

Fig. 6b

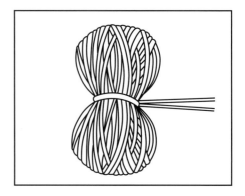

Fig. 6c

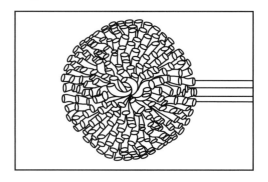

Production Team: Instructional Editor - Jennifer S. Hutchings; Technical Editor - Linda Luder; Editorial Writer - Susan McManus Johnson; Graphic Artist - Amy Gerke; Photo Stylist - Sondra Daniels; and Photographer - Jerry Davis.

Ornaments made and instructions tested by Janet Akins and Marianna Crowder.

We have made every effort to ensure that these instructions are accurate and complete. We cannot, however, be responsible for human error, typographical mistakes, or variations in individual work.

ISBN-10: 1-60140-339-9
ISBN-13: 978-1-60140-339-1